Daniel was always a creative person, even as a child, and enjoyed many activities. He is a new author, an aspiring illustrator, and has several projects he is currently at work on. Daniel is a true believer in Jesus Christ and has been for over a decade now. This book is the first of his works of faith to be published and he is happy to share it with heaven and the world. It's Daniel's love for God that provides his ambition.

DANIEL HEATH STROHM

JESUS HEALS AS SEEN THROUGH THE BOOK OF LUKE

AUSTIN MACAULEY PUBLISHERS™
LONDON · CAMBRIDGE · NEW YORK · SHARJAH

Ordering Information
Quantity sales: Special discounts are available on quantity purchases by corporations, associations, and others. For details, contact the publisher at the address below.

Publisher's Cataloging-in-Publication data
Strohm, Daniel Heath
Jesus Heals

ISBN 9781685626761 (Paperback)
ISBN 9781685626778 (ePub e-book)

Library of Congress Control Number: 2023915909

www.austinmacauley.com/us

First Published 2023
Austin Macauley Publishers LLC
40 Wall Street, 33rd Floor, Suite 3302
New York, NY 10005
USA

mail-usa@austinmacauley.com
+1 (646) 5125767

This book is dedicated to GOD, my One True Love, and for my mother and daughter.

Thanks to Matthew, Mark, Luke, and John. And much thanks to all those at Austin Macauley Publishing who contributed to my book reaching publication.
Thank you all.

When Simon's mother-in-law had a high fever,

They asked Jesus to help and He came and healed her.

And when the sun was setting, people came who weren't feeling well,

But, one by one, Jesus healed them all.

And in the synagogue, there was a
man possessed,

But when Jesus commanded, the evil spirit
came out and left.

And when a leper came to Jesus asking to be seen,

Jesus touched the man, and said: “Be clean!”

And when the paralyzed man was lowered before Him,

Jesus healed him and said, “Friend, your sins are forgiven.”

And even on the Sabbath, Jesus healed a man,

By restoring the man's shrivelled right hand.

And when a centurion's faith amazed the Lord,

Jesus healed his servant with only a word.

And when Jesus saw a widow, with a dead son,

He told her, “Don’t cry,” and raised up the young one.

The Widow's Son

And when the demon, Legion, possessed a man, naked and alone,

Jesus cured him and told him to, "Return home".

And when the woman with bleeding for twelve years, touched his cloak,

She was healed instantly and, “Go in peace,” Jesus spoke.

And when He couldn't get to Jairus' daughter and she died,

Jesus woke her up when all the people cried.

And for the boy with convulsions, whose father was sad,

Jesus healed him quickly and gave him back to his dad.

And when Jesus commanded a mute demon to leave,

The man that it came out of could suddenly speak.

And on the Sabbath when He saw a woman crippled for years,

Jesus healed her and freed her from her pain and her fears.

And when Jesus went to eat at the house of a Pharisee,

He healed a man there who was suffering from dropsy.

And on His way to Jerusalem, Jesus healed ten lepers, all men,

And one of them, a Samaritan, praised God and thanked Him.

JERUSALEM

And nearing Jericho, a blind man cried, “Son of David, have mercy on me!”

He was brought before Jesus, who healed him, and immediately could see.

JERICHO

And when the servant of the high priest lost his right ear,
Jesus touched him and healed him, right then and right there.

Jesus healed many during His Ministry,
Maybe one day He will heal you and me.

Printed in the USA
CPSIA information can be obtained
at www.ICGtesting.com
LVHW050004281023
762383LV00045B/504

9 781685 626761